THE TWO PAGE SPREAD | Where Is

On the cover - Keith Keplinger shot Stacey and Tom Clark's amazing 1983 Mercury Capri - RetroFox. A journey of more than three years from the bottom to the top of the Western Hemisphere. Richard Truesdell captured Héctor Argiró's amazing 1969 IKA Torino. Follow Héctor online at www.elmundoentorino.com.

THE TWO PAGE SPREAD | In Our Words

Moving Forward

Back in September, Keith and I had the opportunity of being interviewed by Dr. Samir Husni, AKA "Mr. Magazine." He is the Professor Emeritus at the University of Mississippi's School of Journalism and the founder and director of the university's Magazine Innovation Center at its School of Journalism and New Media. It was a wide-ranging interview where Keith explained the founding of The Two Page Spread (T2PS), our collaboration in bringing it to print via Amazon/Kindle's print-on-demand platform, and our plans going forward. You can read the entire interview by visiting **bit.ly/T2PS**

Recently, I discussed this interview with a long-time friend and another publishing colleague, Joe Babiasz. Joe and I go back a long way, to 2007 when I did a story on his 1967 Buick GS340 for *Musclecar Enthusiast*. We went back and forth on one of my favorite topics, what is the proper length for a magazine car feature? Keith and I have different views on the subject; short and sweet like we produce here at T2PS versus my thoughts on longer, more expansive features. After sending him some copies of our POD efforts,

he's firmly in Keith's camp, "less is more."

How do you feel about our efforts here? Communicate and share your thoughts with us on T2PS Facebook Page.

Next, Keith and I would like to welcome new contributor to the T2PS ranks, Greg Rager. Greg has worked with each of us, with Keith at Dobbs Publishing, and me at Amos Automotive where we worked together at *Cars and Parts*. Greg is bringing T2PS features from his vast career (see page 14 for his first T2PS contribution) and editing a special project that is coming soon.

Buckle up, the best is yet to come.

Richard Truesdell, Editor, The Two Page Spread

Safety First

Dodge has long been one of the linchpins of the Chrysler Corporation. Its post-World War II lineup was motivated entirely by six-cylinder engines. A V-8 would wait until 1953 when Dodge unveiled its own V-8 engine. It was a development of Chrysler's first-generation Hemi. Dodge marketed as the "Red Ram." With its hemispherical combustion chambers, it produced a stout 140 horsepower from just 241 cubic inches. Unlike second and third-generation Chrysler Hemi engines, it was a fuel sipper, as Dodge beat all other American eight-cylinder engines in the 1953 Mobilgas Economy Run.

At the opposite end of the performance spectrum, this advanced engine set 196 AAA speed records at the Bonneville Salt Flats. It also paced the 1953 edition of the Indianapolis 500.

In 1954, Wally Parks expanded the scope of the three-year-old National Hot Rod Association (NHRA) to legitimize drag racing. NHRA managed its first official race in 1953 at the Los Angeles County Fairgrounds in Pomona, California, and Parks felt the organization was ready to expand its influence.

Working with like-minded enthusiasts, Bud Coons, Bud Evans, *Hot Rod* photographer Eric Rickman, and Chic Cannon, Parks scheduled a 10-race inaugural season for 1954. The organization acquired a 1954 Dodge Coronet Suburban station wagon. It was used to haul an attached a Viking travel trailer full of timing equipment, a public address system, telephones, and a generator, along with associated wiring to power up events during the 17-week schedule in the inaugural season.

After its duties were finished for the 1954 season, the wagon, dubbed the "Safety Safari," was sold. It was replaced with a 1955 Plymouth wagon. Then five decades later, the Pomona-based Wally Parks NHRA Motorsports Museum unveiled a clone of the original, this 1954 Dodge Sport Suburban, restored to replicate the original Safety Safari. Under the direction of the museum, it was restored by the extensive Southern California hot rod community,

While the restoration crew was able to recreate the look of the original, it did receive some

The National Hot Rod Association promoted the sport with a very special 1954 Dodge Suburban station wagon, better known as the "Safety Safari."

Words and photos by Richard Truesdell

significant upgrades beneath the skin. Mopar supplied a 360-cubic-inch crate motor which was backed up with a modern three-speed Torqueflite automatic transmission. Behind the Safety Safari, it now tows a restored Viking trailer, similar to the original. In the almost two decades since it was built, it has appeared at industry events like the SEMA Show as well as promoting the NHRA at venues from coast to coast.

It currently resides at the Wally Parks NHRA Motorsports Museum in Pomona, adjacent to the Pomona dragstrip, home of the Winternationals. The museum is open Wednesdays through Sundays from 10 AM to 5 PM. For more information, call 909/622-2133 or visit www.museum.nhra.com.

Best of Both Worlds

Over the last 30 years, I've written more than 1,500 magazine features so it takes something truly special for a car to stand out. Michael Laiserin's 1964 Chrysler 300K, is one of those cars, one of just 3,022 hardtops produced that model year.

"I came across this car sitting on a trailer in the swap section of the Spring Fling in Van Nuys, California," said Michael. "It was a complete but rough-looking, unrestored car. It was pretty devoid of options as far as luxury cars go, even radio and side view mirror delete. The original window sticker was in a box full of paperwork dating back to before the original owner even purchased the car. He checked off very few options, just leather trim, a Sure-Grip differential, and the '300K special package' which included the dual four-barrel, cross-ram equipped engine. The paper trail even included the paperwork for even custom tuning at the famous Granatelli Automotive. I struck a deal for it and the seller trailered it to my place in Phoenix."

But what makes this particular 300K stand out? A close look under the hood at the car's cross-ram 413 V-8 tells the story. Michael explains. "Having owned my ram engine ragtop for over 20 years, I know that even when tuned properly, you've got to have a feel for how to drive the dual quads. These were built for the open road and they weren't exactly civil for cruising around town. The decision was made to retain the ram induction but to add EFI for driveability."

Classic looks combined with a fuel-injected, bored and stroked 413, and modern creature comforts make this one special Chrysler 300K.

Words and photos by Richard Truesdell

1960s kidney-bean-style wheels.
Overall I achieved the look I wanted
with the car."

While the EFI setup is noteworthy for sure, along with its stealth infotainment system concealed in the dash, the car's overall look sets it apart, making it so memorable. A quick phone call to Michael confirms that even after more than 15 years of ownership, he still owns the car. What could be better than classic looks combined with modern tech? No wonder Michael has no plan to part with it.

"A four-speed manual trans with overdrive would make cruising fun and overcome the 4.10:1 gear needed to launch this heavy beast. A hydraulic roller cam would maximize power and alleviate the need to regularly remove the intakes to adjust the valves. The original KK1 Silver Turquoise paint color was retained as was the black leather interior. I needed to upgrade the wheels as there was no way 14-inch tires were up to the task of maintaining adhesion with the road considering all the weight and power involved here. I settled on 18-inch Centerline Boulevard wheels custom-ordered with unpolished centers and they were reminiscent of the 1950s and

To read the 2018 Mopar Muscle *feature visit* bit.ly/MM1964Chrysler300K or use the QR code.

THE TWO PAGE SPREAD

THE TWO PAGE SPREAD

Rambler

When Is a Rambler American not a Rambler America?

When it's an IKA Torino built in Argentina.

In the early 1960s, American Motors was riding high. In 1962, it was the third bestselling-selling nameplate in America. Its long-time CEO, George Romney—Mitt's dad—had left the company in 1962 to make a successful run to be Governor of Michigan. And in 1963, *Motor Trend* selected the entire AMC lineup as its Car of the Year on the strength of the all-new Classic and Ambassador models.

The third model in AMC's 1963 lineup was its compact American. Its design dated back to the original 1950 Nash Rambler. It was discontinued in 1955, then brought back in 1958. In 1961 it received an angular restyle. For the 1964 model year, it got a complete makeover, sharing many parts with the mid-sized Classic. That version got a restyle in 1966 that carried it to the 1969 model year. In 1970 it was replaced by the all-new Hornet.

The 1964 American was available in two- and four-door sedans, a four-door station wagon, a two-door convertible, and a very attractive two-door hardtop. In 1965, along with other AMC products, it received an all-new optional 232cid straight six. This engine lived on in many forms, including a bulletproof 4-liter version, until 2006 when the JK Jeep Wrangler received the Pentastar V-6 engine.

When the American was reskinned with a more squared-off body in 1966, the tooling for the 1964-65 models was sent south to Argentina, to Industrias Kaiser Argentina (IKA). There it was given new front and rear sheet metal from Pininfarina and was powered by an updated version of the Kaiser OHC six. It was produced until late 1981 when it was the last rear-wheel-drive car produced with a Renault badge.

American?

Words and photos by
Richard Truesdell

The car you see here is a very special first series 1969 Torino 380. It is owned by Héctor Argiró. And I'll let him tell you why it's so special.

"It was the dream of my life, to unite by land the ends of the Western Hemisphere Ushuaia, Tierra del Fuego, Argentina with Deadhorse, Alaska. Since I was a child I looked at the maps imagining the way. I was inspired by my uncle who owned a Torino."

"I started the trip on November 24, 2016 and traveled to 19 countries; Argentina, Chile, Paraguay, Uruguay, Brazil, Bolivia, Peru, Ecuador, Colombia, Panama, Costa Rica, Nicaragua, Honduras, El Salvador, Guatemala, Belize, Mexico, USA, and Canada."

"From March 2020 to November 2021, I suspended the trip due to the pandemic. Returning, I visited New York, Cape Canaveral, Daytona, Savanah, Atlanta, Chatanooga, Pigeon Forge, New Jersey and New York, where I am now."

These photos were taken back in 2019 when Héctor and I connected on his trip north. Given that my first car was a 1965 Rambler American 440H two-door hardtop, it was great to see Héctor's car up close, with the early Pininfarina restyle and the mid-sixties Ferrari-like interior.

Follow Héctor's adventures on his social meda platforms at
🌐 elmundoentorino.com
📘 El Mundo en Torino
▶️ El Mundo en Torino

THE TWO PAGE SPREAD

More is Better

There was a day when folks bought cars to drive, use and enjoy. Pampered concours restorations were reserved for the Model-T Ford crowd, and the Motor City assembly lines were cranking out muscle cars faster than Lucy's candy line. Even a bagboy at the local Piggly Wiggly could be motoring around in more power than most could handle, at prices often in the sub $3,000 range.

Even with brutal horsepower numbers available stock from the factory, many owners chose to – albeit found it necessary to - step things up, personalizing their cars. If factory 'go-faster' parts weren't available, (Direct Connection for the Mopar faithful), the aftermarket was rife with more goodies than your local speed shop could stock all at once. Fuel Injection and computerized engine management systems were viewed as Buck Rogers futuristic dreams. The reality of it was, we could tweak ever more horsepower and performance from our cars, without worry of Big Brother knocking on our door. It was a time we shall not see again, and most enthusiasts today would never understand. It was as if Detroit were selling blank canvases, just so we could create our own works of art.

Robert Vollaro's stock-appearing 1971 Hemi Charger can be quite deceitful, as the 56-year-old retired New Jersey postal worker took the liberty of "tweaking" the Charger's drivetrain a bit – 40 + years ago. Under that massive hood rests a 12.5:1 compression 426 Hemi built by K&G Speed Shop in 1973. The camshaft is a 1968 Race Hemi grind: the Hemi inhales via a vintage Rat Roaster intake manifold mounting original dual Carter AFB carbs. A Mopar Performance Electronic Ignition with a chrome box keeps the fire lit while exhaust headers and Flow Master mufflers assist the elephant in exhaling.

Downstream is a Robert Severino-built, full manual shift, reverse pattern 727 TorqueFlite controlled by the stock Slap Stik shifter. Bringing up the rear are 4.88 cogs in a Dana 60 rear end, suspended by Mopar Performance Super Stock springs. Front tires are factory originals. While the totally streetable Charger appears showroom stock, the 4,200-pound beast runs 11.30/128 mph quarter-mile times, all with 40-year-old technology and an engine that hasn't been apart since it was built in 1973.

You could honestly say Robert Vollaro's 1971 Hemi Charger redefines the term, "Blast From The Past."

Robert Vollaro's 1971 Hemi Charger proves even perfection can be improved upon

Words by Greg Rager, photos by Dave Verna

The 1969 - 72 Mercedes-Benz 300SEL 6.3 is a legendary motorcar, this one is just a bit more epic.

Words by Richard Truesdell,
Photos by Leonard Mayorquin

Shant Meshefedjian has a 90-car collection and owns a body shop as well as CMS Motorsports and Restoration in Southern California. He had added a 1971 Mercedes-Benz 300SEL 6.3, which he said, "This car's first owner was actor and director Peter Fonda and I bought it from his daughter Bridget."

Peter owned the car from 1971, picking it up at the Mercedes-Benz facility in Stuttgart, Germany. Then embarking on a 3,000-mile tour of Europe to promote a just-released movie, *The Hired Hand* in which he directed and co-starred with a well-known American character actor, his long-time friend, Warren Oates. Oates participated in the tour which was fully profiled in chapter 19 of Peter's 1998 autobiography, *Don't Tell Dad*, his dad being acclaimed actor, Henry Fonda.

At the time, Peter was married to his first wife, Susan Brewer, and together Peter and Susan had two children, Justin and actress, Bridget. Peter and Susan divorced in 1974. As part of the settlement, Susan got Peter's beloved 300SEL 6.3. Very little is known of Susan's ownership of the car, but she did transfer the title of the car to her daughter Bridget in 1991, verified by the California DMV records.

Shant acquired the Mercedes when a neighbor brought the car to his attention. Initially, Bridget considered having Shant's shop to put the car back on the road. Ultimately, she decided to sell it to Shant, with just over 16,000 miles on the odometer. Shant happened to be to be in the right place at the right time and he had this to say, "I'd like to say that this car is a keeper. It is the centerpiece of my collection, and I can't imagine ever parting with it."

Check out this video clip of Peter Fonda talking about his lifelong love affair with Mercedes-Benz
https://bit.ly/FondaInterview

THE TWO PAGE SPREAD Star Power!

Read the full story on the Fonda 300SEL 6.3 Mercedes in the Fall 2022 issue of *Classic Mercedes*.
https://bit.ly/CMFondaFeature

We bought the 1973 F100 Ranger from down South in Florida in 2021 from a guy that had most of the work done to the truck already. He was selling it to try to finish another project he had going on. Chris had been looking for a F100 for a while and found it on Facebook Marketplace. We did add Dakota Digital gauges, changed out the transmission bracket, transmission cooler, and replaced the original seat with a F250 bench seat. We love taking the truck for rides around town as a family so Attitude added more seatbelts for all four of us. Being in Florida, the Attitude-installed Vintage Air system was a must. The truck has awesome patina on it, and we like the fact that it's not perfect and don't have to be afraid to drive it anywhere.

Carlee Klaas

Chris brought his truck up from Florida for us to address some overheating issues with both the cooling system and supercharger as well as installing a Vintage Air A/C system, new front accessory drive, oil pump gears, and dyno tuning. What started out as a simple project grew more complicated once we discovered what was supposed to be a Gen 1 engine was actually a Gen 2 running on a modified Gen 1 control pack that was largely unable to be tuned. We swapped that setup for the correct Gen 2 engine control, and corrected other fuel and cooling system issues. The reward was this Gen 2 Coyote/6R80 with a 2.9 Whipple combo laying down a stout 670rwhp on 93 octane and 725rwhp on E85! And, in case you're wondering, those are 24x15s on the rear, with a meaty 405/25-24 tire!

Brandon Conner/Attitude Street Cars

Family Truckster

Chris and Carlee Klaas' 1973 Ford F100 Truck is the perfect vehicle for hauling the family on a night on the town.

Words by Carlee Klaas and Brandon Conner, Photos by Keplinger Designs, Inc. Courtesy of Attitude Street Cars.

It had been relegated to a parts car, and had not run in 15-16 years, when I bought it for $500. It was originally a 4-cylinder turbo engine, 4-speed manual transmission car. I managed to get it running with the original engine and drove it two laps around my neighborhood (about one mile), then I put it on jackstands and ripped the suspension out. Replaced everything with SN 95 components, along with an 8.8 rear end, using 31-spline axles, 3.73:1 gears, and a Ford locker differential.

I drove it in this configuration for about two years and had a blast with it. It had rust around the sunroof the entire time so I decided to change the roof skin and it went from there. The car was stripped to an empty shell and every nut and bolt was addressed. Eighteen months later, the car was painted Ford Ingot Silver/PPG Hot Rod Black, and custom graphics made from a scanned NOS set. We decided to be a little different and stand out, because the car now sports a 500hp 351W engine, T56 Magnum 6-speed transmission, and complete Maximum Motorsports suspension with Koni Yellows and coilovers.

The engine block came from my dad's very first round track race car. He has his doubts that I actually used 'his' engine, but I can assure you, it's the same. It dealt him fits when it was in his race car, and has continued with me, it spun a rod bearing and ate the crankshaft and a couple of rods when it was built and put in my car. It's since been built all over again with a Scat crankshaft and connecting rods. It uses Promaxx aluminum heads, 11.5-1 forged pistons, and the complete Holley Sniper EFI and ignition system. The exhaust runs through BBK longtubes into a Flowmaster two-chamber catback system.

The interior uses Braum seats, Dakota Digital gauges, and a 4-point rollbar. The wheels are SVE Series 3. The decision for the paint color and stripe colors came about one night, sitting with a couple of buddies, talking about the car and having a few frosty brews. Looking at a Natty Light can, we wondered how it would look, being a brighter silver, with blue stripes, the rest is history.

The entire concept became 'What would it be like, if Ford built it now' concept. The original 3 Pace Cars didn't have any type of warning lights (they used flags on the rear bumpers), but being today's concept, I had to have lights. The Whelen Liberty bar came from a killed-to-death Dodge Charger police car that was going through a salvage auction. I changed all the pods to amber and put in new lenses.

The car is happy now, setting the pace from the Brickyard to the show field.

Setting the Pace

Jason Lawley's 1979 Mustang Pace Car went from parts car to pacing the world of Mustangs

Words by Jason Lawley, photos by Keplinger Designs, Inc.

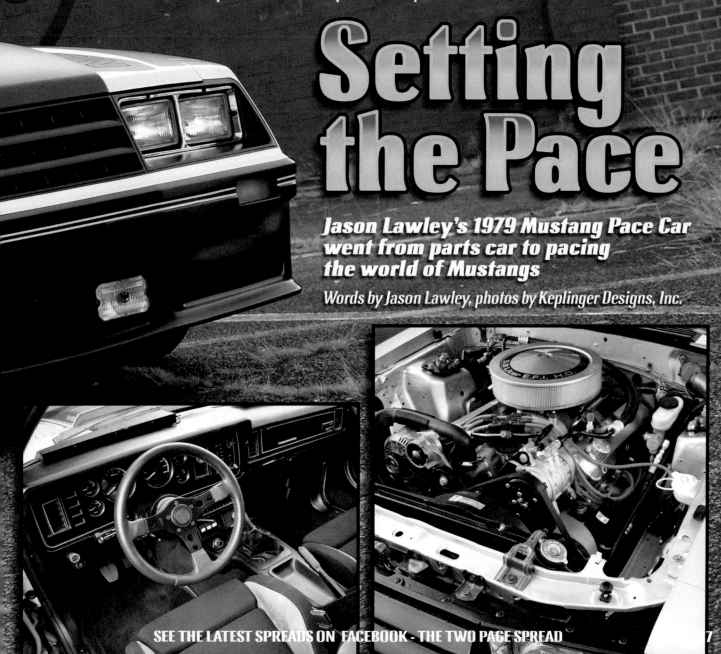

THE TWO PAGE SPREAD — Never Lift

This Kremer K3, which won the 1979 24 Hours of Le Mans, remains the Holy Grail of the 935 series.

Words and photos by Richard Truesdell,

Bruce Meyer is an automotive Renaissance Man. The affable California real estate investor and entrepreneur is best known as the founding chairman and motivating force in the establishment of the Petersen Automotive Museum. Meyer is also the chairman of the annual Father's Day Rodeo Drive Concours d'Elegance, which has evolved into one of the world's great car shows. But if Meyer is known for anything, it's the fantastic car collection that he's assembled and curated over the past five decades. One of the crown jewels of his collection is a 1979 Porsche-Kremer 935 K3, the overall Le Mans winner in 1979, acquired in a swap with the Indianapolis Hall of Fame Museum. To give you insight into Meyer, he lives by the words, "Never Lift."

The 935 was a byproduct of the era where the rules, such as they existed, were made to be stretched and ultimately broken. In the case of the 935, introduced in 1976, it was built to compete under the FIA-Group 5 rules, required production-based cars utilizing doors and windows in their original stock position. But beyond that, just about everything else was left wide open to a liberal interpretation of the rules.

One of the issues that the powerful, turbocharged 935 presented was how to get the car to handle properly. A reported half-million Deutschmarks was spent developing the rear spoiler, designed to keep the rear end planted in the corners. But the increased drag was a liability when it came to straight-line speed. Porsche designer Norbert Singer saw a huge loophole in the liberal Group 5 rules. This allowed the replacement of the stock-appearing 911 front clip with flat-style bodywork which would become the visual trademark of the 935 and would work in harmony with the rear spoiler. Next, enter the Kremer Brothers, Manfred and Erwin.

Starting in 1977 Porsche offered the 935 to non-works teams. For the 1978 season, Kremer built the K2 which enjoyed a degree of success. But the K3 was built for the 1979 racing season that literally turned the Kremer Brothers' creation into a world-beater, putting the K2 on a weight-saving diet, much of it courtesy of composite (mostly Kevlar) bodywork.

A lot of the car's notoriety, 43 years on, comes courtesy of two of its three drivers. The primary driver was Klaus Ludwig, with co-drivers Don and Bill Whittington of Florida. Their rise is subject to a lot of speculation concerning the distribution of recreational pharmaceutics which I discuss in more detail in the full feature I wrote back in 2014 for *Total 911* in the UK.

For a YouTube interview with Bruce Meyer and his collection, visit bit.ly/BruceMeyer935 or snap this QR code.

For a link to the full Total 911 feature, visit bit.ly/Porsche935Feature or point your device to this QR code.

Shortly after Mustang Week 2018, my wife Stacey really wanted an early Fox-body Cobra as she had fallen in love with the color combo and graphics on Mike Clay's 1980 Mustang Cobra. After a few months of searching and coming up empty handed, I mentioned "what about a Capri RS?" After seeing some pictures, she immediately fell in love with the bubble hatches. The search was on for a 1983-86 Capri. In short order, we found this 39,000 mile 1983. The things that checked the boxes on this car for us were the factory 5.0L engine, 5-speed transmission, A/C, low mileage and white interior.

From there we started trying to figure out how to give the Capri that retro flare like Mike's Cobra. We named the car RetroFox, designed some custom retro graphics that were inspired by the Mercury Capri Pace Cars from 1985-86. A set of turbo fan-inspired 18" 3SDM wheels were then modified for the car to help keep the retro theme going but also with a nod to a vintage motorsport look. The interior got completely overhauled back to stock appearing with the help of new white seat upholstery from TMI.

Once the visuals were taking care of, it was time to focus on the chassis and suspension. Everything under the car has been rebuild or upgraded. We

RetroFox

Stacey and Tom Clark redefine 'Retro' with their 1983 Mercury Capri

Words by Tom Clark, photos by Keplinger Designs

threw the Stifflers catalog at the car starting with the FIT System subframe connector setup to help stiffen up the car. Coilovers came from the guys at Raceland so we could get the stance dialed. The car was updated to a 5-lug setup and Cobra spec brakes. The rest of the suspension was upgraded with adjustable pieces from UPR Products, so we could get stance that the car now has.

Under the hood, the focus was to clean it up and make it mechanically sound and trouble free, including making sure that A/C blew ice cold. After all, this car was built to cruise at Mustang Week, so cold A/C was a necessity. With some bolt-ons under the hood, a carb rebuild and tune, mods to the

intake, and a Flowmaster exhaust system, it all helped the 5.0L breathe a little bit.

The car's first showing was at Mustang Week 2019, the year the show was cancelled due to Hurricane Dorian. Luckily we still were able to make a showing at the Retro Meet - which let's be real, this car is truly at home at the Retro Meet. At the 2021 Retro Meet, Vaughn Gittin, Jr stopped and talked to Stacey and I about the car and told us it was by far one of his favorites from the event, and that he could see the intent of what we were trying to build. So being able to debut the car at Retro Meet and then the following year hearing the kind words from Vaughn about the car, is what it is all about for us, it's been a blast.

THE
TWO
PAGE
SPREAD

JR CARR

TERI CARR

REAL PRO STOCK

PDRA
PROFESSIONAL DRAG RACERS ASSOCIATION

"I was distracted," said JR Carr, after a run at a National Hot Rod Association (NHRA) Mountain Motor Pro Stock Event in Indianapolis - that comment was shocking. How can someone be sitting on the starting line, at a national event, and be distracted? In mid-to-late 2020, there certainly was a lot to be distracted by, but really, on the starting line? After hearing this, we were seriously concerned in the Real Pro Stock studios.

That concern was alleviated, when he delivered a 6.179-second, 228.23mph hit later in the year at the NHRA St. Louis event. JR Carr was now the Quickest and Fastest Mountain Motor Pro Stock driver in history—he was first in the teens. So, 2021 was setting up to be an exciting one, with that kind of performance, correct? Only time will tell...

The Professional Drag Racing Association is the place JR Carr normally races, so finishing second in the 2020 Championship Points to Johnny Pluchino must have been a bitter-sweet pill, but JR is all class and was in Johnny's pit, to congratulation him and the team, at the 2020 Season Closer at Virginia Motorsports Park (VMP).

Carr was heavily favored in 2021 Real Pro Stock Power Rankings, but floundered during the first four races, his reaction times were simply lacking. He

A Tale of Two Seasons

Following up on the improvements at the end of the 2021 season, JR Carr grabs the #1 ranking in 2022.

Words by Scott Soucy, photos by Tara Bowker. Presented by Real Pro Stock.

qualified number one, at all but one 2021 event, but simply couldn't seal the deal in those first four races. He was almost nine rounds out of first place—it seemed like 2021 was over. Then, he won the first two races of the second half of the season and the narrative completely changed, reaction times were improving—there was a little swagger.

2021 Champion Chris Powers brought a new car into the field, which, in our humble opinion offered the distraction that Johnny Pluchino (who was also struggling on the low-end of his runs) and JR Carr needed to gain some ground on Chris Powers, who started the season with a crucial PDRA Season Opener win at GALOT Motorsports Park (Benson, NC).

The last four races were magic, as the charge that JR Carr was staging, placed more and more pressure on Chris Powers. Chris eventually clinched the championship after a first-round victory at the Season Finale at VMP.

That late-season charge is the main reason Real Pro Stock has ranked JR Carr number one on the Real Pro Stock Power Rackings—we wish all the Mountain Motor Maniacs the best in 2022 and simply cannot wait to see what they have for the fans.

Third Time's the Keeper!

Gary Fowler has owned his father's 1973 Bronco three times, this time it's for good.

*Words by Gary Fowler,
photos by Keplinger Designs, Inc.*

My father, James Wilson Fowler, bought this 1973 Bronco new from A. G. White Ford in Cartersville, Georgia, on December 4th, 1972. I ordered one in mid-1973. Six months later it still had not come in (sounds kinda like today). So, in 1974, Dad sold it to me.

In 1975, I sold it to Mr. and Mrs. Satterfield in White, Georgia, for $4,000, and bought it back from Mrs. Satterfield in late 2008 for $4,600. It needed a lot of work but the body was sound.

I took it to my friend John Wilson to do all the bodywork. It was taken all the way to bare metal and took three years to complete. Another friend, Glenn Teague, did all the powertrain work. It was all original, but needed to be completely reworked. In 2017, Glenn bought it from me, and did a lot of upgrades.

I bought it back in 2020, so I have owned it three times. I still have all the original Owner Manuals, including the Warranty Card with Dad's name on it, too.

This Bronco now lives in Cartersville, Georgia, back with me where it belongs.

Special thanks to Dennis Graham for the use of his beautiful property in Euharlee, GA.

Gary Fowler's 1973 Ford Bronco

Kelly and Joe Charles' 2022 Ford Bronco

The RetroMod Bronco

Words by Kelly Charles, photos by Keplinger Designs, Inc.

> *"...doing Bronco things and loving every off-road minute of it."*

Kelly and Joe Charles take their 2022 Ford Bronco where no other new Bronco has gone before – The Past.

"Is that an old Bronco?" is the number one question Joe and Kelly Charles hear when they're out and about in their 2021 Bronco Badlands. After clarifying the model year, they always proudly exclaim, "The fact that you asked means we accomplished our mission!"

Their mission? To modify their brand-new Antimatter Blue two-door to resemble a late 80's Bronco with as much retro charm as they could pack onto a 30+ year newer model, hence the "RetroMod" title it has since gained. Having to wait an excruciating 568 days from reservation to receipt allowed plenty of time to plan and order parts.

As soon as their Bronco arrived in February 2022, the Charles' added Wimbledon White paint on the sides, top, and roll bar for the classic two-tone look. They fabricating a carbon fiber piece for the top to give the illusion of a slanted body line. Then they had the experts at Glasslife Atlanta cover the entire vehicle in xPel Stealth PPF for a matte finish. Inside you'll find BuiltRight MOLLE panels in the rear, providing the perfect system to secure all the offroad gear.

Other immediately noticeable mods include plenty of KC HiLites (both because they're cool and because they're Kelly's initials and she wouldn't hear of any other lighting product), JCR Offroad Vanguard bumper, Warn winch, and Hammer Built Modular Tailgate Support system with RotopaX fuel container. Underneath, discerning eyes will be quick to notice the King adjustable coil-over shocks, Baja Kits control arms, and 17-inch Method wheels with General Grabber 35-inch red-letter tires. No major engine modifications are planned, although Joe did add a J&L Oil Separator to keep the intake clean.

But the best part of this build? Joe and Kelly's love for the North Georgia mountains has them well away from civilization and anything resembling a paved road several times a month, doing Bronco things and loving every off-road minute of it.

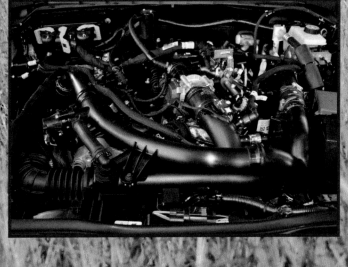

THE TWO PAGE SPREAD

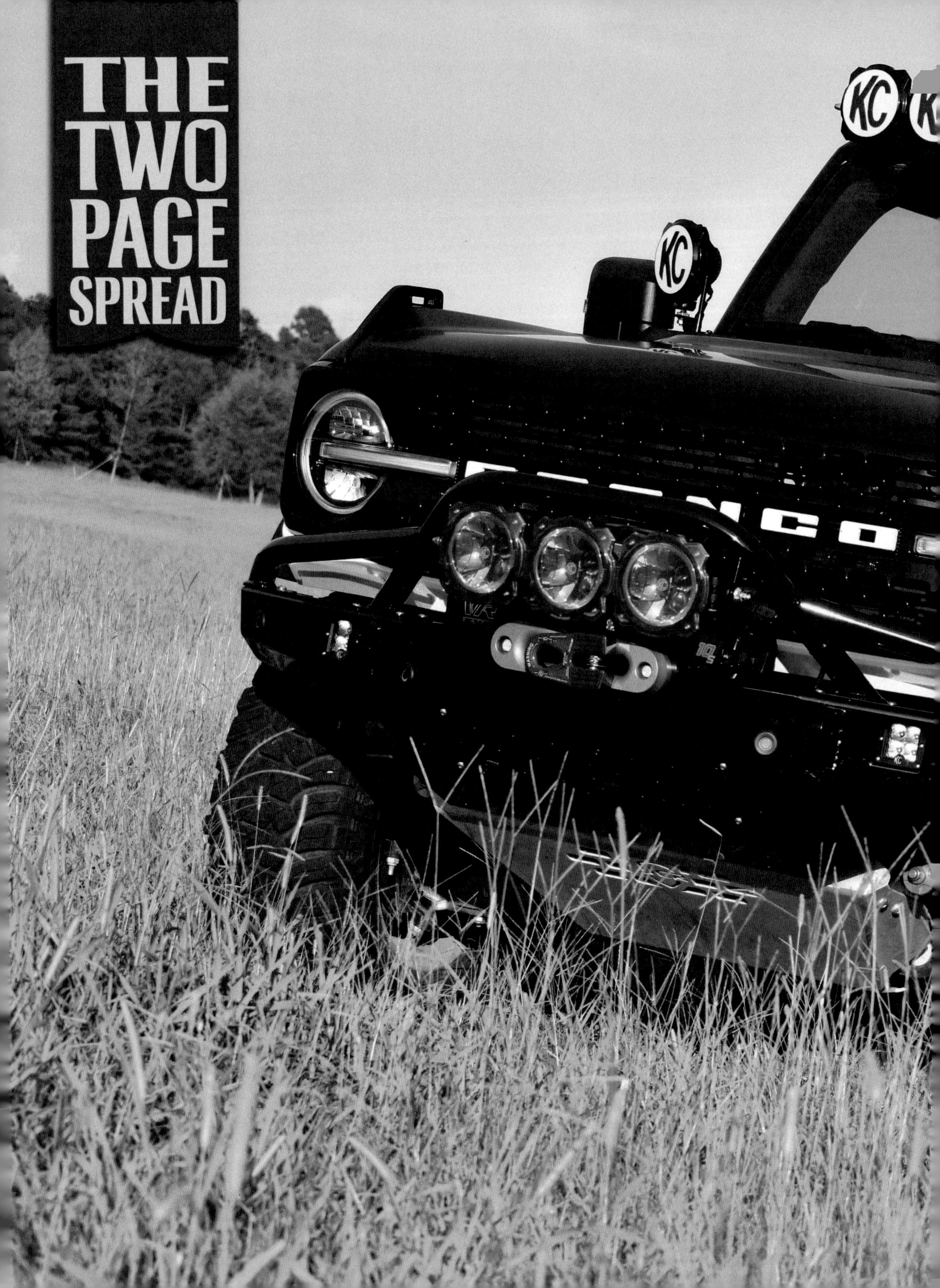

3 Great Books!
by Richard Truesdell & Mark Fletcher

Hurst Equipped
8.5" x 11" • 192 pages

1969 AMC Hurst SC/Rambler B-Scheme

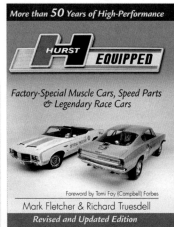

More than *50 Years of High-Performance*

HURST EQUIPPED

Factory-Special Muscle Cars, Speed Parts & Legendary Race Cars

Foreword by Tomi Fay (Campbell) Forbes

Mark Fletcher & Richard Truesdell

Revised and Updated Edition

1970 Maximum Muscle
9.95" x 11.25" • 176 pages

Pontiac GTO "The Judge"

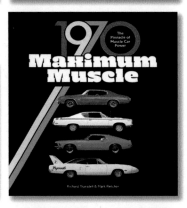

1970 Maximum Muscle

The Pinnacle of Muscle Car Power

Richard Truesdell & Mark Fletcher

Hemi Under Glass
8.5" x 11" • 176 pages

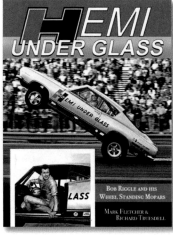

HEMI UNDER GLASS

BOB RIGGLE AND HIS WHEEL STANDING MOPARS

Mark Fletcher & Richard Truesdell

The Two Page Spread Contributing Editor Richard Truesdell has co-authored, with Mark Fletcher, three automotive books over the last decade; *Hurst Equipped* (2012 hard cover, now out of print, 2020 paperback), *1970 Maximum Muscle: The Pinnacle of Muscle Car Power* (2021), and *Hemi Under Glass: Bob Riggle and His Wheel-Standing Mopars* (2021).

Each is a collaborative effort between the two veteran gearheads and are recognized as among the definitive volumes in each category. *Hurst Equipped* pulled from long hidden Hurst archives and interviews with key company personnel.

1970 Maximum Muscle was a true collaborative effort between Rich and Mark, where Mark's extensive research uncovers long-lost factory information with Rich contributing most of the photos from his archives shooting for magazines such as *Musclecar Enthusiast, Muscle Car Review, Chevy Enthusiast, Mustang Monthly,* and many more ex-Petersen/ Source Interlink/The Enthusiast Network titles.

Their 2021 book *Hemi Under Glass* comes from one-on-one interviews with Bob Riggle and recounts his 60 years associated with the legendary Hurst Hemi Under Glass. It also features photos, many never before seen, from Bob's personal archives.

All three books are available from the authors as signed editions; $50 for *Hurst Equipped*, $60 for 1970 *Maximum Muscle*, and $60 for *Hemi Under Glass*, which also signed by Bob Riggle.

See Mark and Rich's 2012 appearance on Jay Leno's Garage at **bit.ly/HurstEquippedBook**

and Mark's 2021 appearance on Jay Leno's Garage with his 1970 AMC Javelin featured in 1970 Maximum Muscle at **bit.ly/1970JavelinLeno**

Get Yours Today!
To order signed copies, contact Rich at richtruesdell@gmail.com or 951/229-2989.
Unsigned copies are available at Amazon.com, BN.com, Autobooks-Aerobooks.com,
and most retailers and booksellers nationwide.